Wandering Woman: Southern California

The Ultimate Road Trip: One Woman's Journey Across the United States by Car

Julie Bettendorf

Contents

Introduction

"Not all who wander are lost." JRR Tolkien

Are you sure? I thought to myself, as I tried not to panic. I was a long way from anything familiar, but that was how it should be. I had driven thousands of miles on dusty, pothole-filled roads. It's often on the worst roads that you can discover something truly amazing.

My dusty CRV was parked beside me, containing one restless dog and a variety of snack bags, all empty by now. There were no buildings in sight, no cars or people or movement at all. Only the constant humming of the insects as they buzzed around my head.

I turned to my left – another straight road that trailed off into the distance. I glanced over to the right, then behind me – two more barely discernible roads stretched out into the abyss. I was in a four-way intersection with no signs, no sense of direction, and no sign of life for several miles. No cell service either. *Damn*, I thought. *I'm lost.*

How did I get here? I couldn't help but feel like this little intersection was a cruel metaphor for life. I began to daydream, imagining each road might transport me back to a different time, a different role in my life, and a different me.

If I took the road from whence I came, it could lead me all the way back to Oregon, back to my cheating third husband, back to a life of loneliness and solitude. There is no greater loneliness than being married to someone who isn't actually present in your life.

If I took the road to my left, perhaps it could take me back to my career as a dental hygienist, a job I hated deep down in my soul. There is something so disengaging about cleaning teeth for a living. It's a disgusting, smelly way to get a paycheck. It pays well, which is great, but the best part is the huge gob of friends I enjoy to this day.

Or maybe the road to my right, *yes – maybe that's the path*, I imagined. Maybe it could take me back to my real treasure, my kids. Back to their smiling, innocent faces as toddlers, as they danced around the Christmas tree and their father and I were still married. Back when they still needed me for every little thing.

But, that was just it. I didn't feel needed anymore. My kids weren't toddlers anymore – they were both full-grown adults, and far too busy for me. My dental buddies were still working, but I wasn't. Dental hygiene had robbed me of the cartilage in my fingers, giving me severe, disabling arthritis. And, I wouldn't be returning to any more husbands either, because three marriages were quite enough for me.

All three of these paths, all three of these roles – the wife, the mother, and the dental hygienist – had seemingly been stripped from me within a year. I was lost and looking to find myself again.

The funny thing about this phrase, "not all who wander are lost" – is that, in my experience, wandering and being lost walk hand-in-hand with one another, and the expression can be flipped. In my experience, not all who are lost are wandering, and that is a real disservice to the beauty and clarity that the world has to offer.

When one becomes lost, wandering is the only option to guide oneself back to a path. After all, one could not come upon any dirt path at all without wandering.

I began wandering at an early age, both with my mind and with my feet. At eight years old, I was reading a book about archaeology and dreaming of one day seeing Egypt. I didn't follow a traditional path in high school either, going heavily into foreign languages, in hopes of one day using them.

At twenty-five years old, I divorced my first husband (the dental student who talked me into becoming a dental hygienist so I could work for him) and decided to give traveling a real shot. I took off for the Andes and Macchu Picchu, climbing up ancient Inca stone steps to reach the magnificent ruins.

Anyone who has been to Macchu Picchu will tell you there is something ethereal and deeply spiritual about the place. The ruins stretch out across the emerald green mountains, way up in the middle of the sky. Macchu Picchu gave me my first experience of feeling history. This trip inspired me to come back and complete a degree in archaeology, and I've been wandering ever since.

More travel followed including a backpack trip around Europe for three months, by myself, and trips to Britain, Italy, and Greece. I visited the burial places of Crusaders, mummies, and ancient kings. I happened upon the castle of my namesake in Bettendorf, Luxembourg, and wandered my way through European history.

My favorite excursion by far was finally seeing Egypt with my daughter in 2012. Just like my childhood dream envisioned, I rode a camel beneath the pyramids of Giza, with my head wrapped in some man's sweaty turban. It was perfect.

Traveling has always been my own personal antidote to pain. I went to Mexico after my first and second divorces, Canada after my third, and Italy after my dad died. Call it avoidance if you want, but I call it an accelerated form of healing in the purest sense of the word. I believe travel can heal your soul.

Wandering has always worked its wonders on me – made me feel renewed, rejoiceful, grateful, and purposeful. It's been my medicine.

So, as I stood in that intersection, I once again wondered how wandering had led me so astray this time. *What the hell am I supposed to do now?* It was then that I realized that one last path had not been considered yet – the path which stretched straight out in front of me. *Which role does this represent?* I pondered.

The answer smacked me in the face.

That last dirt road – the only path that could take me where I wanted to go, the only path that ever truly healed me or showed me the way – was the path of the traveler. The wife, the mother, and the hygienist roles – though valued in their time – were sitting in the bleachers now. It was time to welcome and enable my boldest, bravest, and perhaps most pivotal role yet:

The role of the Wandering Woman.

Welcome to Wandering Woman

This book is for you – the grieving empty nester mom, the begrudged housewife, the woman in need of a drastic change in her life. Really, this book is for anyone with a passion for traveling. If you feel lost with no sense of direction or purpose in life, that's a bonus – this book will be even more appealing to you. And lastly, if you're a man reading this book, congratulations for holding a book with the word woman in the title. You're contributing to gender equality, and that's pretty neat.

I decided to combine three of my dearest loves – travel, history, and archaeology – and put them into a book because I believe wandering has the power to change your life. I have been to many areas of the world and had too many outstanding experiences to list. However, by the time both my children had

Me

moved out in 2017, I had never seen my own country – America. It was the perfect time to explore a new country (my own) and discover a new me at the same time.

So, I packed up my Honda CRV, along with some gear and my 14-year-old furry friend, Sadie. *Wandering Woman* is the chronicle of my journey across eleven states, discovering the joy of getting lost and finding myself along the way.

Why America?

A merica, the beautiful? I sure think so, but I didn't realize just how beautiful our country is until I embarked on traveling across eleven western states in a year.

The United States offers everything for the discerning palate. From spectacular beaches, austere mountains, to rolling plains, our country has it all. It's difficult to comprehend just how large and impressive our scenery is, until you experience it first-hand, with the ultimate road trip.

I also realized just how much of our history is missing from U.S. history I was taught as a kid. The history of our country didn't begin with the pilgrims landing on Plymouth Rock in the 1600s. Our history is far more ancient, with rock art and archaeological sites dating back over 12,000 years.

We also owe a tremendous debt to early pioneers who tamed our land. The Mormons and other groups ventured into the great unknown with their families and their worldly possessions. Some of them pulled cumbersome handcarts across the country to settle in inhospitable, dangerous locations.

The goal of Wandering Woman is to bring history back to life and make it interesting again. I am presenting some famous sites, and many little-known ones. You will take the road-less-traveled with me, while we explore ghost towns, rock art sites, archaeological sites, and museums, to discover the colorful tapestry that is our country.

I present some history, including dates, but my goal is to present more of the real-life stories of history, including ghost stories, profiles in history, voices from the past, and moments in time, to give you, the reader, a deeper understanding of the context of history.

This is by no means an exhaustive list of places to visit. In fact, I encourage you to discover America for yourself, as I did, by making a trek across the land by car. You can explore as the early explorers did, just a little more comfortably, with a lot less hardship.

I hope you enjoy this book and take a little time out to discover our beautiful country, and maybe even discover yourself in the process.

Safe Travels,

Julie Bettendorf

Welcome to Southern California

The Golden State

Southern California has something for everyone, and everyone knows it. It's a populous area that still retains its historic charm and beauty. From the great beaches to the great cities, Southern California has it all. California is truly the golden state.

5 things to love about Southern California:

- Spectacular Spanish missions like San Antonio de Padua

- Miles of gorgeous coastline and sparkling beaches

- Fabulous historic buildings like Hearst Castle

- Great museums like the Getty Center

- Wonderful walkable areas like Old Town San Diego

Dreams of Southern California

"*As one went to Europe to see the living past, so one must visit Southern California to observe the future.*" **Alison Lurie**

"*As a photographer, God's light in Southern California is something unlike I've ever seen on planet Earth. There's a beauty about it, especially in the afternoon that is so pretty.*" **Marty Stuart**

"*I first saw the ocean as a kid. We would drive from Arizona in the summer and arrive as the sun was starting to come down over the hill near Laguna in southern California. We would always sing a song, and it was a big joyous family moment when we came over the hill.*" **Ted Danson**

Top Stuff to See in Southern California

Favorite Museums:

- Getty Center, Los Angeles
- Museum of Us, San Diego

Favorite Historical Sites:

- Hearst Castle
- La Brea Tar Pits

Favorite Spanish Missions:

- Mission San Antonio de Padua
- Mission San Miguel Archangel

Favorite Way to Spend an Afternoon:

- Walking around the San Diego Zoo

Early Southern California

Early San Diego

Early Picnic in La Jolla

Early Excavations at La Brea Tar Pits

Mission San Antonio de Padua

The ***Mission San Antonio de Padua*** was founded in 1771 and is California's third mission. It lies within the boundaries of the Hunter-Leggett Military Complex.

A sacred space surrounded by military seemed a bit surreal to me, but the mission is a very peaceful place, nonetheless.

The mission contains rooms furnished sparely, with their own simplistic beauty. The mission also contains a large wine cellar to house the wine made at the mission.

The grounds of Mission San Antonio de Padua are spectacular and well-tended. On the cemetery grounds, there is an olive tree and an oak tree, both planted in 1850, and at the time of my visit, they had grown to a majestic maturity.

As I was walking around the grounds, two sweet little black kittens began following me around, and one became trapped inside the church. It took some time to get him to come out.

The museum contains many artifacts including an original missal book from the 1700s. A Padre named Buenaventura Sitjar was a linguist who stayed at the mission for 57 years, working tirelessly on a 400 page book of vocabulary and grammar of the local Indian language. Mission San Antonio de Padua

How to get to Mission San Antonio de Padua:

Mission San Antonio de Padua is located near the town of Jolon, at 1 Mission Creek Road.

Ghost story:

A miner from the gold fields sought help from an Indian woman who lived nearby to nurse him back to health. He fell in love with her and married her, giving her a present of a beautiful white horse. He left to go back to mining his claim, with the promise of returning back to her in a couple of months.

He lingered a bit too long at the gold fields, and when he returned, he found his wife with someone else. In a fit of rage, he killed them both with an ax. Recalling the Indian's belief that a body had to be buried whole, or it would never find peace, he decapitated her and took her head with him. He also killed her beautiful white horse. A phantom headless woman riding a white horse has been seen by several people, including a group of soldiers who followed the apparition, chasing it in a jeep. [Senate]

Voices from the past:

" The Indians of this mission are totally distinct from those I have hitherto seen." **Padre Pedro Font, diarist on the De Anza expedition, March 6, 1776. Padre Font recorded the site as "Mission San Antonio in the Valley of the Oaks."**

A word about the California Missions:

During the years 1769 to 1833 Franciscan priests established a network of 21 Spanish missions, stretching from San Diego to San Francisco, a distance of 600 miles. The function of the Spanish missions was to bring Christianity to the indigenous peoples, and to protect Spanish interests in what was known as Alta California.

18 of the 21 missions were founded by Father Junipero Serra, and Father Fermin de Lasuen, both of whom are buried at Carmel Mission. Other priests involved in the founding of the missions were Father Jose Ramon Abella, Father Jose Altimira, Father Pedro Benito Cambon, Father Estevan Tapis, Father Luis Gil y Taboada, Father Vicente Francisco de Sarria, and Father Narciso Duran.

Hearst Castle

Publishing magnate William Randolph Hearst started building his glorious *Hearst Castle* near San Simeon, California in 1919. He would spend 28 years building and adding to the amazing castle on the hill. When Hearst Castle was finally completed, it would boast a staggering 130 rooms, full of priceless antiques and works of art from around the world. The main building, Casa Grande, has 115 rooms including 38 bedrooms, a library, movie theatre, kitchen, and living quarters for the household.

Many rooms of the castle contain spectacular tapestries, which transport you back to the Medieval period. Hearst was a collector, and the entire house and grounds are filled with priceless artifacts and antiques from the ancient world.

My favorite features of Hearst Castle are the pools. The indoor pool features over 1 million Murano glass tiles, some with gold leaf inside. The Neptune Pool has a seventeenth century statute of Neptune and Roman columns from the first through fourth centuries. California State Parks

Take your time strolling the grounds and enjoying the spectacular view.

How to get to Hearst Castle:

Hearst Castle is located on the Central California coast, near San Simeon at 750 Hearst Castle Road.

Profiles in history:

William Randolph Hearst was born April 29, 1863 and began to run the San Francisco Examiner newspaper at the age of 22. He would grow what became a vast publishing empire, with 28 newspapers and 18 magazines. He also dabbled in film making, creating more than 100 films. Hearst was an enigma, becoming a democratic representative, once running for president, supporting FDR, and also supporting the Nazi movement at one point.

Hearst suffered during the Great Depression, liquidating many of his assets in the 1930s. It's lucky for us that Hearst was a collector, using his wealth to accumulate vast amounts of ancient artifacts from all over the world. He also bought entire furnished rooms from historic buildings in Europe, and had them shipped to his estate. Hearst was an important figure in the preservation and restoration of the Spanish Missions, especially Mission San Antonio de Padua. Hearst died in 1951 at the age of 88.

Mission San Miguel Archangel

The ***San Miguel Mission*** was founded in 1797 by Father Fermin Francisco de Lasuen, and it became the 16th of 21 missions. Each of the twenty one missions is a day's travel away from the next mission on the trail. _{Mission San Miguel}

It's also one of my favorite missions, because of the impressive collection of artifacts housed within it. Each room is a miniature museum. The San Miguel Mission has many interesting rooms including the Padre's bedroom, which has sheepskin windows.

The Mission Church, built in the years 1816 to 1818, has original walls hand painted by Esteban Munras, an artist and a Salinan Native American. The paints were made of minerals mixed with cactus juice.

The grounds of the mission are gorgeous and rustic, and it is a joy to walk around and see the wooden gateways and meandering paths. You can see remnants of the orginal stonework, including the bell tower. Walking through the picturesque, well-tended cemetery is a serene experience. It has an early burial from 1798.

As you walk around the mission grounds, don't miss the Cross of El Camino Real, the Royal Road which connected the California missions. The road was marked with a cross carved into the bark of a tree. The bark would grow back in later years, covering the carved cross. This tree fell, uncovering the carved cross beneath the bark.

Just across from the San Miguel Mission is the Rios-Caledonia Adobe, built in 1835. It was used in 1868 as an inn, hotel, stagecoach stop and a tavern. The Dalton brothers, and Frank and Jesse James all visited it. Rios Caledonia Adobe

How to get to San Miguel Mission and Rios Caledonia Adobe:

The San Miguel Mission and Rios Caledonia Adobe are located in the city of San Miguel at 775 Mission Street.

Ghost story:

During the time of the gold rush, the mission was run by John Reed, an Englishman, who operated it as an inn. He amassed a fortune and hid it on the mission grounds.

The inn was attacked in 1849 and John Reed, along with 13 men, women, and children were murdered. They were buried in a mass grave in the mission cemetery. Visitors feel cold spots when they visit the mission and the figure of a lady in white has appeared. The figure is thought to be John Reed's wife. Senate

Mission San Luis Obispo de Tolosa

Mission San Luis Obispo de Tolosa was founded September 1, 1772, and became the fifth Spanish mission in California. The original builder of the mission, Father Jose Cavaller died in 1789 and is one of three priests buried in front of the church altar. The large front door of the mission was designed so that horses could pass through, so the horses wouldn't be stolen. The door can be seen in the museum. The door also contains a special "kitty door" through which cats could pass. The cats kept the mice and rats under control.

The patron saint of the mission is St. Louis of Toulouse, who was born in France in 1274. His father was Charles II the king of Naples. Louis renounced his claim to the crown to join the Franciscan order at 22. Louis died of illness at age 23.

The museum is wonderful, containing entire rooms of period furniture and artifacts.

This is the room of the Padre, containing only a small table, chair, and bed.

One of my favorite pieces is a 19th century carved bone and ivory triptych depicting Christ's time with the disciples and Mary Magdalene, and the arrest of Christ.

Another old piece is the Alcalde's chair. The Alcalde served as the Mayor of each town. This chair is handmade out of cowhide, and is from the 19th century.

My favorite piece in the museum is this fragment of the mission sundial, found in 1928. The sundial dates back to 1796.

The mission grounds are tranquil and serene, so breathe deeply as you enjoy the calm surroundings

How to get to Mission San Luis Obispo de Tolosa:

Mission San Luis Obispo de Tolosa is located at 751 Palm St. in San Luis Obispo, California.

La Purisima Mission

La Purisima Mission is the 11th of 21 missions, and was founded by Father Fermin de Lasuen in 1797. It is known by its full name of Mision la Purisima Concepcion de Maria Santisima, which translates to Mission of the Immaculate Conception of Most Holy Mary. It's a serene place with beautiful, spacious grounds. It's one of my favorite missions because of its pastoral setting and how immense it is. What makes it even more appealing is that it is out in the middle of nowhere. It is a destination all by itself.

The mission was damaged during the 1812 earthquake. Spain stopped support of the missions during the Mexican War of Independence from 1810 to 1821. The mission was taken over when California became a state in 1846. La Purisima contains many rooms and buildings, so take your time. The furnishings are minimal, recreating the difficulties of mission life.

La Purisima was not without its comforts, including the wonderful library. The mission was a busy place, with rooms dedicated to candle making, saddlemaking, weaving, and cooking.

La Purisima has expansive grounds, including the cemetery, which contains hundreds of Chumash and Spanish, buried after 1821. Father Payeras is buried under the altar in the church. He served La Purisima from 1804 to 1823. California State Parks

How to get to La Purisima Mission:

La Purisima Mission is located near Lompoc, California at 2295 Purisima Road.

Ghost story:

There is a building at La Purisima Mission that was once a jail. This building is said to be haunted by the ghost of a young vaquero who was murdered by another man.

It seems the two were in love with the same woman and one of the men lured the other into the building, stabbed him to death, and buried him beneath a section of wall. His ghost is said to produce the icy feeling many experience when they enter the building.
Senate

Santa Barbara
Mission

The ***Santa Barbara Mission*** was established on the feast of Saint Barbara on December 4, 1786, by Father Fermin Francisco de Lasuen, because Padre Serra died two years earlier in 1784, before he could establish the mission.

Father Lasuen later left Serra's companion in charge, Father Antonio Paterna. The current building was constructed in 1820 because the previous structures were badly damaged during the 1812 earthquake. The church architecture was taken from the Ten Books of Architecture, written by Roman architect Vitruvius in 27 BC.

The cemetery contains the graves of at least 4000 Indians, including some graves which date back to 1789. One of the burials is that of Juana Maria, a young girl who was abandoned. The stone skulls above the door were used to represent a cemetery. Senate

How to get to Santa Barbara Mission:

The Santa Barbara Mission is located in the city of Santa Barbara at 2201 Laguna Street.

Profiles in history:

Juana Maria was left behind on the island of San Nicolas when the Indians evacuated. She lived alone on the island for 18 lonely years before she was eventually rescued.

She was taken to the Santa Barbara Mission, but she lived for only a few weeks. She died in 1853, and is buried in the cemetery of the Santa Barbara Mission. She is the subject of the book Island of the Blue Dolphins.

Santa Barbara

El Presidio de Santa Barbara State Historic Park was built in 1782, and was the last of four presidios built by the Spanish in California. The presidio functioned as protection against English and Russian incursion into the area. The Presidio is an active archaeological site, with current excavations uncovering the cooking area, and an aqueduct.

The Chapel was the hub of social events for the presidio. Residents came to pray three times each day. Next to the altar, paint was used to convey the look of tapestries and other luxuries. There are fifty-one people buried under the chapel floor.

Each family living in the presidio had one small room with an attached yard.

The Canedo Adobe is one of the two structures which survives from the original fort. The building was deeded to Jose Maria Canedo, during the American Period. Canedo was a descendant of the soldiers who settled the area.

El Cuartel is the second of the two surviving buildings, and it functioned as a guardhouse. It is also the oldest building in Santa Barbara. A main reason why El Cuartel survived is that it was continuously maintained and lived in by Presidio soldier Jesus Valenzuela and his descendants, who lived there until 1924.

How to get to El Presidio de Santa Barbara State Historic Park:

The Santa Barbara Presidio State Historic Park is located at 123 East Canon Perdido Street, in Santa Barbara.

Voices from the past:

"I once traveled with a party of New Yorkers en route for California... They soon learned that champagne, East India sweetmeats, olives, etc. etc., were not the most useful articles for a prairie tour."
from The Prairie Traveler by Randolph Marcy, U.S. Army, 1859.

Mission Basilica San Buenaventura

The ***Mission Basilica San Buenaventura*** is in the vibrant old town section of Ventura, California. Founded March 31, 1782, the mission became the ninth of the Spanish missions in California. An unusual feature of the mission is a seven-mile-long aqueduct which was constructed by the mission residents. The aqueduct provided water to the residents from the nearby San Buenaventura River.

The residents planted gardens and orchards, which grew in abundance, thanks to the new water supply. English Captain George Vancouver visited the gardens and described them as the finest he had seen. Mission Basilica San Buenaventura

The mission was controlled by the Mexican government, beginning in 1834. When California became a state in 1850, the Catholic church petitioned the United States government for the return of the mission. In 1862, President Abraham Lincoln gave the mission back to the Catholic church.

My favorite artifacts in the museum are the original wooden bells, dating from 1782. The wooden bells don't have clappers, leading historians to believe the bells sounded when they were hit with a stick. Mission Basilica San Buenaventura

How to get to Mission Basilica San Buenaventura:

The mission is located at 225 E. Main Street in Ventura, California.

Pasadena

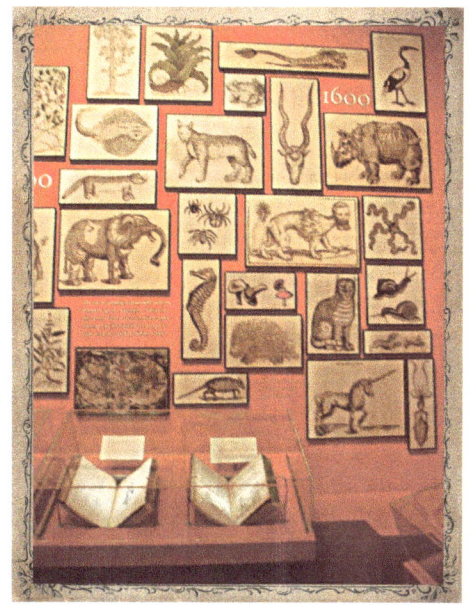

The **Huntington Library**, Dibner Hall History of Science, is
a must-see if you love science. It is divided into four sections:
Astronomy, Natural History, Medicine, and Light. As I walked in,
I felt as though I was where knowledge began.

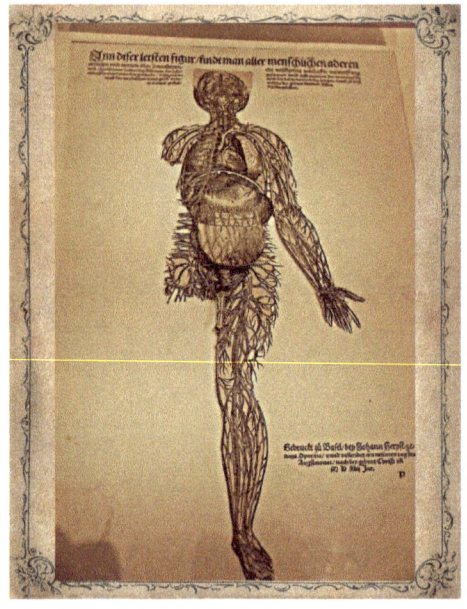

My background leads me to be fascinated with medicine, so this section was especially rewarding for me. The medicine section has the groundbreaking work, "Epitome" by Andreas Vesalius from 1543, with overlays used by 16th century medical students to learn anatomy.

The other sections offer their own masterworks by Galileo, New-
ton, and many others. There are many, many famous works, all
in one building, including an original illuminated Gutenberg Bible
from 1433, and an illuminated volume of Chaucer, from 1405.

One of my favorite pieces is an account of The Battle of Chesapeake, during the Revolutionary War . It was written in 1781 by Pierre-Joseph Jeunot. The illustrations of the sailing ships are truly masterpieces. Don't miss an original Audubon Birds of the World, and an original Shakespeare from the 1600s. Huntington Library

How to get to the Huntington Library:

The Huntington Library is located near the city of Pasadena, in San Marino at 1151 Oxford Road.

Mission San Gabriel Archangel

The ***Mission San Gabriel Archangel***, in the San Gabriel area of Los Angeles, is the 4th of 21 missions, founded in 1771. The mission walls are original, and are over 4 feet thick. The roof and ceiling were damaged in 1804 and again in 1812 by earthquakes.

The baptistry is also original with a copper font, and silver baptismal shell brought from Spain in 1771. The church pulpit is original, with an altarpiece made in Mexico City and brought to the mission in the 1790s.

There is an original chest of drawers in the sacristy which is made without nails. The vestments are from the 1600s and the bedroom set is from 1623.

There are many books housed in the mission, with the earliest dating from 1489. There is also a Bible, printed in 6 volumes on sheepskin, in Venice, Italy, 1588. San Gabriel Mission

The mission grounds are lovely, with a perfect composition of bright flowers and plants. The cemetery was consecrated in 1778, and 6000 Indians are buried there.

How to get to Mission San Gabriel Archangel:

The Mission San Gabriel Archangel is located at 428 S Mission Drive in San Gabriel

Voices from the past:

"On our arrival, they killed 4 sheep, whose meat was good. I do not remember having eaten mutton more fat and tender, also chicken. All of us loved San Gabriel Mission. Its fat cows that give rich milk from which cheese and butter was made."

As Father Paterna says, "It is like the Promised Land." **Father Font, dairist to the De Anza expedition, on stopping at the mission on the way to become the first residents of San Francisco. January, 1776.**

Los Angeles

Los Angeles has a very unusual fossil site, known as the ***La Brea Tar Pits***. It's exactly where you wouldn't expect, right in the heart of Los Angeles, on some prime real estate. This area of primeval ooze is now surrounded by modern buildings.

Over 5 million fossils have been removed from the pits, covering a period of the last 55,000 years. Two of my favorites are the mammoth and sabre-tooth cat.

Among the many superb museums in Los Angeles, one stands out; it's the ***Getty Center***, perched high on a hill, providing sweeping views of Los Angeles. The museum contains collections from oil magnate J. Paul Getty. Walking through the center is like being on a 3D chess board, with multiple levels, called "pavilions." It took me awhile to find anything, but the hunt was well worth the effort.

The collections include illuminated manuscripts, ceramics, paintings, and applied arts from before 1600 to after 1800, arranged in four buildings. [Finch]

One of my favorite individual pieces is this exquisite silk room divider. The details, including numerous vibrant parrots, make this an exceptional piece.

There are also complete, paneled rooms, from the 1600s to the 1800s, like this one. It's a spectacular French paneled room, dated to about 1790-1795. The ornate panels are all hand-painted by several famous artists of the period.

This pilgrim flask from Venice, dated 1500-1520, shows two boys holding a blank shield between them. Prospective owners could apply their own coat of arms to the shield.

The Getty Center has a little something to delight everyone, in-cluding this compound microscope and case, from France, dating to about 1751.

How to get to Los Angeles historic sites:

The La Brea Tar Pits are located at 5801 Wilshire Blvd

The Getty Center is located at 1200 Getty Center Drive

Profiles in history:

Jean Paul Getty, or J. Paul Getty, as he is more commonly known, was born in Minneapolis, Minnesota in 1892. He came from wealth. His father, George Getty, was an oil millionaire. J. Paul Getty made his fortune by buying up independent oil companies, becoming a billionaire in the 1950s. He was married five times, and had five children.

Getty was known to be a miser. He installed a payphone for members of his staff and visitors to his English estate. Getty had the reputation of being the richest man in the world when he died in 1976. The Getty Center houses J. Paul Getty's impressive collection of masterpieces in painting, sculpture, manuscripts, decorative arts, and furniture.

Mission San Juan Capistrano

Mission San Juan Capistrano was founded in 1776, by Father Junipero Serra. It is the 7th of the 21 California Missions.

The Mission has the original walls of the chapel where Father Serra held mass. The massive original walls provide some idea of the imposing nature of the mission.

Take your time strolling the grounds and exploring the rooms of this beautiful, historic place.

How to get to Mission San Juan Capistrano:

Mission San Juan Capistrano is located at 26801 Ortega Hwy in San Juan Capistrano.

A word about the swallows coming back to Capistrano:

Father O'Sullivan served at Capistrano from 1910 to 1933. One day he saw a shopkeeper swatting down swallow nests. The priest is said to have told the swallows *"Come on swallows, I'll give you shelter. Come to the Mission. There's room enough for all."*

The swallows started building their nests at the mission. So every March 19th, St. Joseph's Day, the swallows come back to Capistrano.

Mission San Luis Rey de Francia

The **Mission San Luis Rey de Francia**, near Oceanside, is known as the King of Missions, for its majestic size. The mission became the largest building in California by 1830. The mission was founded on June 13, 1798, by Father Fermin Lasuen, and became the 18th of 21 Spanish missions in California.

It was named after King Louis IX of France, who lived in the 13th century. He was compassionate toward the poor and often served food to them himself. He died in 1270 and became a saint in 1297.

One of my favorite pieces in the museum is a magnificent carved door. The museum contains a document signed by Abraham Lincoln in 1865, returning Mission San Luis Rey to the Catholic Church. Previously, the mission was owned by the new state of California from 1850. The cemetery dates back to 1798. Early settlers, friars, and indigenous people are buried there.

In front of the mission, you can see the ruins of the soldier barracks, which were once the home of Spanish soldiers who protected the mission. Later, the soldier barracks were home to American soldiers during the Mexican-American war of 1846 to 1848.

The mission has a nice little coffee shop, from which you can gaze at the oldest pepper tree in California. Seeds were planted in 1830, growing into the large tree seen today. From the same viewing platform, you can see the original carriage arch, once part of a large arcade containing a kitchen, workshops, a hospital, dormitories, and other support buildings.

How to get to Mission San Luis Rey de Francia:

Mission San Luis Rey de Francia is located at 4050 Mission Ave in Oceanside, California.

San Diego

San Diego has so much to offer, so I will begin with one of the most pleasant ways to spend an afternoon, walking through the ***Old Town***. Its many excellent eateries, shops, and historic sites make Old Town San Diego a destination all by itself.

You can start with the ***Machado and Stewart House***, an adobe structure built in 1835. The house looks comfortable, with intricate stencil work on the walls. Outside, the grounds are spacious, inviting, and shady.

You can't miss the **Whaley House**, a famous structure, popular with paranormal enthusiasts. The house was built in 1856 by Thomas Whaley, who stated, *"I feel I will have the nicest house in San Diego."*

The house served several purposes while the Whaley family were living there. The structure served as a courtroom, a theatre, a general store, and the Whaley's living quarters, all at the same time.

Theatre productions at the Whaley House cost 75 cents for a reserved seat, or 50 cents at the door. ^{Whaley House, Glass}

Along with original furnishings throughout the house, there are several interesting artifacts, including a small vest pocket pistol, once owned by Lillian Whaley. It was found in 1951, in a neighbor's yard. Lillian was a librarian, who carried the pistol with her. Apparently, it was common practice at the time for librarians to carry protection.

Ghost story:

The Whaley House, in San Diego's Old Town, was described by Life Magazine and others as *"the number one most haunted house in America"* because of the many ghosts and supernatural phenomena experienced there. There were several hangings on the spot, before the house was built on the site.

Some of these unfortunates, including a man named "Yankee Jim Robinson" have been seen at Whaley House. Yankee Jim was hung for grand larceny back in 1852. The house is also said to have Thomas Whaley himself haunting the place, along with Violet Whaley, who committed suicide in the house in 1885. Glass

Don't miss the ***Maritime Museum***, with its star attraction, the Star of India. It's the oldest active merchant sailing ship in the world, beginning its journey on November 14, 1863. The ship has served many functions in its lifetime, including hauling jute from India during the cotton shortage of the Civil War, and transporting immigrants to New Zealand.

A very beautiful Hollywood set is here too. It's the HMS Surprise, the replica sailing vessel used in the Master and Commander movie. The HMS Surprise is a copy of a British Navy Warship, built in the 1700s.

Another important vessel is the Berkeley Steam Ferry, the first steel-hulled ferry to operate on San Francisco Bay. She helped evacuate residents during the 1906 San Francisco earthquake.

There is a steam yacht from 1904, the Medea, and a B-39 Russian submarine, used during the Cold War. It's a sobering experience climbing inside the cramped quarters, which once held 78 men, and went down to a depth of 985 feet.

Another beautiful ship on display is the San Salvador, a replica of Cabrillo's Spanish Galleon which came into the bay in 1542. San Diego Maritime Museum

When you visit San Diego, **_Balboa Park_** is a must-see. The park was built in 1868 and contains some fine museums, and the world-famous **_San Diego Zoo_**, a delight for animal lovers, and everyone else.

The San Diego Zoo began its history in 1915 by housing exotic animals left on their own after the Panama-California Exposition. Today, the zoo houses over 4000 animals on 100 acres of land.

One of my favorite animals is there. It's the rare Okapi, the only living relative of the giraffe. There are walk-through areas which get you right up close to the animals.

There are several ways to see the park, including by bus, gondola, and hot air balloon. Personally, I recommend walking it as much as you can. You don't want to miss anything.

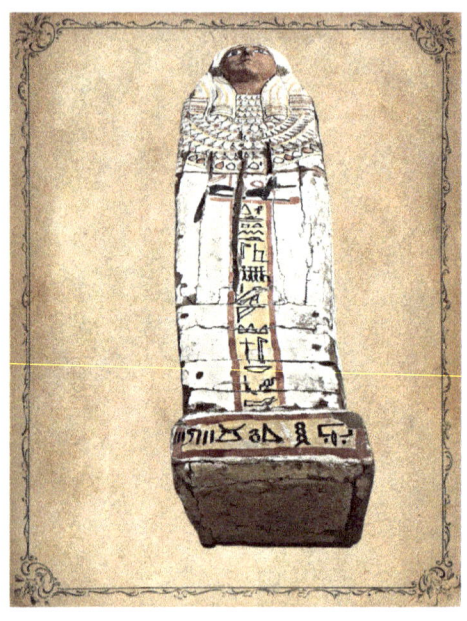

Another don't miss site in Balboa Park is the ***Museum of Anthro-pology,*** known as the ***Museum of Us***. Ancient cultures includ-ing the Maya, Moche, and Inca are well represented.My favorite section is all about Ancient Egypt, and includes fine examples of sarcophagi.

I love the details on the pieces, including Anubis, my favorite little black jackal of the underworld.

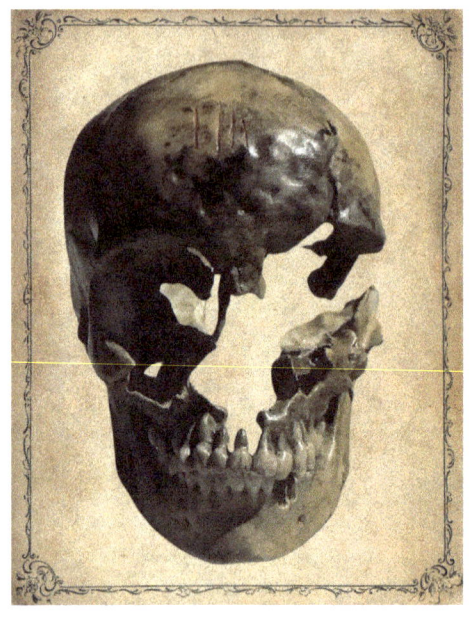

The Museum of Us contains a wonderful collection of everything that tells our story, including a fascinating bit of information about cannibalism among the Crusaders. According to three sources, during the 1098 siege in Syria, the Crusaders butchered, cooked, and ate the bodies of their enemies.

Other historic incidents of cannibalism are detailed, including an account of finding human remains during the 2012 excavation of Jamestown. Among the remains was a mutilated skull and leg bone of a teenage girl. The remains indicated she had been cannibalized during the winter of 1609-1610. Digital imaging and 3D printing have been used to recreate the beautiful girl she once was.

Historical accounts of cannibalism also include the whaling ship Essex, immortalized in Moby Dick. The ship was sunk by a whale and the crew escaped in small boats. The men began by eating the dead, and then ate an unfortunate cabin boy who drew the short straw.

You can end a wonderful day in San Diego with a visit to the *Cabrillo National Monument*, where Juan Rodriguez Cabrillo landed on Sept. 28, 1542. He named the bay San Miguel, because Saint Michael's feast day was coming up.

How to get to San Diego historic sites:

The Machado and Stewart House is located at 2707 Congress Street.

The Whaley House is located at 2476 San Diego Avenue.

The Maritime Museum is located at 1492 N Harbor Drive.

Balboa Park is located at 1549 El Prado.

Cabrillo National Monument is located at 1800 Cabrillo Memorial Drive.

Profiles in history:

Juan Rodriguez Cabrillo, was the first European to explore the west coast. His mission was to map the coast, establish trade with China, and find a non-existent passage from the Pacific to the Atlantic oceans. Born in 1499, he grew up in Seville, Spain. He sailed to Panama, and arrived in Cuba in 1517-1518. He became part of Hernan Cortes' party, serving as a crossbowman during the conquest over the Aztecs in Tenochtitlan.

He also joined Conquistador Pedro de Alvarado on an expedition into Guatemala. Cabrillo became commander of the flagship San Salvador. Along with two other ships, the La Victoria, and San Miguel, the three ships contained officers, crew, slaves, and priests. They entered San Diego harbor on sept. 28, 1542. He named the bay San Miguel, after the patron saint's feast day. He then went north to what is now Los Angeles, and up to the Channel Islands, where Cabrillo suffered an injury.

Cabrillo died of complications and infection from the injury on January 2, 1543. A carved stone was found on Santa Rosa Island in 1901. The stone is etched with a cross, a stick figure, and the initials JR, and is believed by many to be the gravestone of Cabrillo. The journals of Cabrillo didn't arrive in Spain for 16 years, and when they did arrive, the Spanish government officials decided that since the area was not full of gold, they would not go there again. Thus, the coast of California was not explored for 230 years. The Spanish eventually returned, establishing many of the Spanish missions in locations first marked by Cabrillo.

Mission Basilica San Diego de Alcala

The ***Mission Basilica San Diego De Alcala*** was founded July 16, 1769 by Franciscan Priest Father Junipero Serra. It's the first of 21 missions that spread upward through California.

The church was destroyed in 1775 by an Indian attack. Father Luis Jayme was killed during the attack and became the first Christian Martyr in California. He is buried at the mission.

Padre Serra rebuilt the mission in 1776, installing defensive walls around it. The grounds of the mission are wonderful and well-tended, so take your time to fully enjoy them.

Don't miss the Padres' living quarters, consisting to two rooms. In 1850 to 1857, the U.S. Military used the mission to house soldiers, and these two rooms were converted into housing for the senior military officer's family.

How to get to Mission Basilica San Diego de Alcala:

Mission Basilica San Diego De Alcala is located at 10818 San Diego Mission Rd.

Favorite Places to Camp

San Mateo Campground at San Onofre State Beach in San
Clemente has 157 campsites all of which have fire pits and picnic
tables. There are also full hookup sites available. There is an
RV dump station, showers, and flush toilets. The campground is
dog-friendly, with lovely grassy meadows, and lots of squirrels
and bunnies. The campground also has a 1.5 mile trail leading
to Trestles Beach, a mecca for surfers. For reservations go to
www.parks.ca.gov.

Anza Borrego Desert State Park Campground is a wonderful area for enjoying Southeastern California. The campground has 120 campsites, many with full hook-ups. The campground is dog-friendly too. You can also enjoy dispersed camping in the over 600,000 acre wilderness area. For more information, visit ***parks.ca.gov***

Random Thoughts
What History Means to Me

First, let me start by sharing with you my opinion of what history isn't. History is not a collection of random dates, names, and places for you to memorize. History is not a dry and uninteresting class you have to pass to graduate.

I believe history is a tangible thing. You can actually *feel* history in the places you go, and the sights you see. I remember walking up to the Acropolis in Athens. I looked down at the well-worn marble steps and wondered about how many ancient philosophers had climbed these very steps, thousands of years ago.

You don't have to go far away to experience the *feeling* of history. If you are lucky enough to live in an old house, you may experience history in your own surroundings. You might say to yourself, *"If only these walls could talk."*

During my travels across the United States, I *felt* history in many, many places. If you travel across the country like I did, you will *feel* the wonderful history of our beautiful country for yourself, and you will never be the same. You will discover what it means to be an American.

Why I did it and why you can too:

I decided to travel across the country by car because I wanted to rediscover America. When I first set out to explore the history of our country, I wanted to find out why America is the greatest country on earth, and what it means to be an American.

The politics of these United States was frightening at the time. Our country was polarized, almost beyond repair. Whether it was Democrats or Republicans, Conservatives, or Liberals, everyone was fighting.

I wanted to rediscover the joy of being an American. I wanted to rediscover our rich history, our unique and wonderful people, our tapestry of multicultural heritage, and our rich natural resources. I thought a road trip by car across eleven western states was a good place to start.

I have a degree in Archaeology, and a passion for all things archaeological. I love history, with a side love of paleontology. It is these three passions that I set my trip agenda around. I set out to discover the archaeological sites, history, and paleontological world of our country.

As I travel and write my books, I get asked all the time, especially by women, "What is it like to travel by yourself? Aren't you scared?" The truth is, I believe everyone should do what I did. It's a wonderful way to discover our country, and to rediscover yourself. The truth is, I'm scared not to travel. Traveling allows you to get to know yourself, in ways not possible when sitting on the couch watching TV.

We tend to spend a lot of our lives tuning out the world and our place within it. When you travel, you are quite literally forced to deal with your own thoughts, emotions, and feelings. You can discover yourself while traveling. You can come to understand what makes you who you are, and how you can perhaps become a better person. Above all, traveling gives you mental clarity to figure out how to live with intent. It's a way to guide your life, not just wait for things to happen.

Travel Tips & Stuff
What You Need to Know

How to get started:

P lanning your trip should be one of the most exciting things about it. You want to be spontaneous, but it is also very wise to plan your route, so you can take full advantage of all the time and miles you will invest.

- First, decide your passions. If you love airplanes, trains, or old vehicles, plan your trip around that. If you love gardens or architecture, seek that out as the focus of your trip.

- Next, read and research areas of the country that will let you enjoy what you are interested in.

- Make a list by state and city or town, of what you want to see.

- Take your handy road atlas and locate the areas on the pages.

- Make a tentative route plan, so you have an idea of where you are going.

Travel tip: Avoid trying to plan your trip down to a schedule of days, hours, or minutes. On a road trip, it will be virtually impossible to know where you will be on any given day. If you adhere to a schedule, you are more likely to stress out, and less likely to actually enjoy yourself, which is the whole point.

What you need:

You need to bring along a sense of adventure and a curious mind. You need to ditch the idea of always being on a schedule, and live a little more spontaneously to thoroughly enjoy yourself. Things will happen as you travel, both good things and bad things, and you need to prepare your mind and your soul for day-to-day changes.

So much of our lives are planned out. Between growing up, going to school, finding a career, marriage, kids, or whatever, people have lost much of the ability to be spontaneous. But you must take spontaneity on the trip with you, because you may make detours along the way to see something really spectacular.

So, for the practical stuff you need:

A great vehicle-I have a Honda CRV which is fabulous. It's old, a 2004, fully paid for, and will go anywhere. I see humongous RVs on the road, towing a car behind, and all I can think of is, they can't go just anywhere. They are too big. Bad gas mileage, cumbersome to drive, slow, and not agile like my CRV. So, I encourage you, if you want to go car camping and be able to go on remote dirt roads, get an agile vehicle, and Hondas are great.

Travel tip: Don't be afraid to do some modifications to your vehicle. I took one of my back seats out. (after watching a YouTube video) I threw in a twin mattress, a bit of drapery, and some netting. I also put some of those little portable light switches on the inside. I jettisoned anything I hadn't used up to that point. Don't be afraid to get rid of unnecessary stuff.

An awesome camera that you know inside and out. I use a Nikon and it takes wonderful pictures. Don't skimp on a camera, and don't think a cellphone camera is all you need, because you want the best for your beautiful photos.

A hot plate warmer-this little item was indispensable. You need a converter for it so you can plug it in to the cigarette lighter. Place your food inside it, carton and all, and then plug it in. 30 minutes for thawed food, about an hour and a half for frozen food. Boom! You have a hot meal by the time you stop for the night!

Window shades-the best ones are magnetic so you just place them against your windows and they cling to them, obscuring the view inside your car.

Portable cooler with wheels-another indispensable item that works great and is easy to move around. I use those nifty blue frozen blocks in mine.

Portable air compressor-this little gem plugs into your cigarette lighter and will inflate your tires if you have a flat. Fortunately, I haven't had to use this yet.

Portable battery charger and power bank-mine comes with battery cables and the power bank, yet once inside the case, it is small enough to put in your glove compartment. This little item, unfortunately, I have had to use, and it saved me.

Portable generator-mine came with a small solar panel, so it can be charged with solar or electricity. It has a decent battery life and also doubles as a light for night-time.

All season clothing-you never know what different states will bring for weather, so take hot weather and cold weather clothes, and a fair amount of shoes appropriate for hiking, or walking, sandals, and slippers, which are nice at night. Also take along a pair of cheap rubber flip-flops to wear in the public showers you might go into.

Your own pillows-I like my own pillows, so I don't wake up with neck cramps, especially after sleeping in the car.

Sleeping bag and cozy blankets-you want to stay warm and layering is everything.

Warm hat, warm socks, and fuzzy jammies to keep you warm for cold nights sleeping in the car.

A great road atlas, and great guidebooks-get one that's easy to read, with great pictures. For a road atlas, just get one that is easy to read.

A word about photography:

Along with a great camera, you need to have a great eye. This is easier than it sounds once you have worked with your camera and are comfortable taking pictures with it. I am not a professional photographer, but I like my pictures and other people do too.

These are my tips for taking great pictures:

- Experiment with taking both horizontal and vertical shots.

- Don't always put the subject of the photo in the middle of the photograph.

- This one is important: pay attention to the foreground,

and if possible, have something, a plant or whatever, in the foreground to help give the photo dimension and depth.

- This one is important too: turn around often to see the view you just came from. I do this quite often and some of my best pictures have resulted from when I turned around and took the shot.

You can also take a mental photo. Place an image in your mind that you can call upon later. Use all of your senses to see, hear, smell, and maybe even to taste, what is around you. You have the means to fully experience your surroundings, and that is very important to a traveler. When you take a mental photo, be sure to jot down quick little details about what you saw, heard, smelled, or tasted, so you can jog your memory later.

And last, but not least...don't be posing in front of everything, everywhere, to show that you actually went somewhere. Most people want to see themselves in your photo and be mentally transported there, but they can't if you are there already.

To camp or not to camp:

Car camping is great. I prefer it to sleeping on the cold, hard ground in a tent. I can lock the doors, put my window shades up and be cozy for the night.

That being said, for me there were some do's and don'ts about camp sites. Some people camp in a Walmart parking lot and feel safe. I do not. I believe that if you are in a busy area, you're more likely to be confronted by a nut job who may bother you. Nothing against Walmart.

Same goes for casino parking lots. Many people believe that if they are in a public place, there is less chance of someone bothering them. I don't share this belief. I believe you are safer parked out in the middle of nowhere in the dark. That same nut job who can find you in a parking lot is not about to go driving around on dirt roads to see if anyone is parked there. At least that's my belief. You may not share it, and that's fine. Park and camp wherever you feel safe.

I don't go for rest areas either because they have a track record of incidents happening to people in rest areas, especially women travelers.

So, where do I camp? In state or national campgrounds, wildlife sanctuaries, or off on a dirt road somewhere, usually out in the middle of nowhere.

There are definitely times when I stay in a motel. I use Hotels.com because I like their stay 10 nights, get 1 night free deal. So, I book a hotel or motel if:

- The weather is too hot or too cold, or too rainy

- I am in a city and plan to stay awhile

- I'm tired of camping, need a shower, or my body hurts

- I need to do laundry

---⋇---

A word about safety:

When you are a woman traveling alone, it's critical to keep a low profile. Don't tell people you are traveling alone, where you are staying, or any other personal information.

I don't go to bars or get drunk. I'm not preaching but you are on your own, in a city or town you've never been to, and you don't know anyone, so it's not the time to lose control of what you are doing. When you are in control, you are better able to decide which people you want to get to know better.

Travel tip: If you feel vulnerable traveling alone, that's OK. Vulnerability is part of passion, and traveling is a passionate thing to do. You can put one of those family stickers on your vehicle to indicate to others that you are not traveling alone, which can help you feel more secure.

Maintain your connections:

When you are traveling alone, there is a definite sense of disconnection. It feels almost like you are the only one in the world, traveling through space and time. That's why it's critical to keep your connections to loved ones active.

Be on Facebook while you are traveling. You may not have internet a lot of the time, or the internet will be poor. Consider paying to have your phone be a hotspot. It's a little bit of money per month, but it's worth it and has saved me from being without internet. I love the convenience of it, and you will too.

Plan your journey around visiting family members or friends you haven't seen for a long time, or people that are good friends. When you see people you know, it will ground you, so you can continue traveling.

Check in by phone with loved ones. They worry about you, and it's good for both of you to stay connected no matter where you are.

Consider traveling with a pet. I started my trip with my beloved 14-year-old sheltie named Sadie. She didn't make it to the end of the trip. I lost her to bladder cancer about four months in. My Sadie was special, and I will never forget my first traveling buddy.

It took me a solid year to decide on getting another dog. I poured over profiles of rescue dogs, looking for a little buddy I could take care of. Best Friends Animal Society in Kanab, Utah, had my perfect match. I now have Rosie, an 8 year-old sheltie that looks just like Sadie and has many of the same mannerisms. Life is good again.

I highly recommend Best Friends Animal Society if you are looking for a pet. They have 3000 acres and house up to 1600 animals at one time including dogs, cats, horses, pigs, and just about everything else. The dedicated people at Best Friends are wonderful both to you, and your potential pet.

Travel tip: One of the easiest and best ways I stay connected while traveling is to offer to take a photo for someone I don't know. Many couples, families, or singles would love to have more pictures of themselves traveling. It's an easy and quick way to have a connection with a fellow traveler, and it's good manners too.

⸺⋖✦⋗⸺

Practical matters:

You need to have an address to send your mail to. Keep in touch with whomever is nice enough to do this for you.

You will also need to come back occasionally to register your car, vote, go to doctor visits, and take care of any other business. You can't leave it all behind, as tempting as that may be.

Bad things that happened:

Remember when I said you need to take spontaneity with you on your trip? Well, there were many times when I used my spontaneity skillset.

The government shutdown happened smack dab in the middle of my travels. That meant that all of the National Monuments were closed. I did a lot of driving and circling around.

I also did a lot of circling around trying to avoid natural disasters. I traveled through Paradise, California shortly before a massive fire happened there. I tried to travel through the area again but was pushed out by massive flooding. My latest event was camping in Canyonville, Oregon and waking up to flames creeping down the hillside. That was day one of the Canyonville fire.

Besides being driven out by natural disasters, sometimes I was driven out by rude people. Many times it was centered around my furry traveling companion. I believe there are really only two types of people, those who love animals and those who don't.

When people see me walking my beautiful, sweet, elderly dog, they either come up and pet her, or they say something harsh.

One incident was a woman, a total stranger, who came up to me smiling down at Sadie and asked how old she was. I replied, "She is 13 and a half years old." The woman replied very curtly "She needs to be put down." Sadie was walking around, alert, and happy, and yet this woman wanted me to end her life because she was old.

Speaking of animals, several times I came very close to driving into an animal on the road. I can't stress enough how many times this will happen to you, and all I can say is, be alert at all times while you are driving. When you travel a lot of miles, you will get tired, so stop and smell the roses, and try not to drive at night.

Good things that happened:

One of the sheer joys of taking a road trip is the unpredictability of it. You never know what you will see. I am originally from Oregon, and bears are not a common sight. So, while driving high up in the Blue Mountains, I looked over and saw a bear! So exciting! He didn't stay for long, kind of shy, but so cute. I love animals, so to see the rich and wonderful amount of wildlife in our country gladdened my heart.

I met many great people on my trip, from all walks of life. They were a walking, talking advertisement for our beautiful country. I smiled at them, and they smiled back. We are all Americans, and we are all part of the human race. When you meet people across the country, you realize just how important it is to get to know your fellow citizens, and learn more about how they view the world and our country.

I have to give a special shout-out to the many dedicated people, often volunteers, who staff our state and national parks and monuments. They work tirelessly to ensure the health of our natural resources, and help travelers enjoy their visit. The same is true of the many people who staff the museums in small towns and large cities. They enjoy history, like I do, and it shows in their smiles.

Along with wonderful people, I have seen an America that is spectacularly beautiful, with open prairies, majestic mountains, and crystal clear rivers. I have seen a small fraction of the history of our country. I have seen the memorials to the brave people who shaped our country. I have fallen in love with America in a way that was not possible sitting in my living room. People ask me, "would I do it again?" The answer comes easily, "Yes, in a heartbeat."

Bibliography & Further Reading

Beautiful Science Ideas That Changed the World, The Huntington Library.

Cabrillo, National Park Service

Carey, John, *Eyewitness to History*, Harvard University Press, 2003.

Enss, Chris. *Object, Matrimony: the Risky Business of Mail-Order Matchmaking on the Western Frontier*. Globe Pequot Press, 2013.

Finch, etc. al.., Jackie. *Eyewitness Travel USA*. DK Publishing, 2017.

Glass, Dean. *The History & Mystery of the Whaley House*. Our Heritage Press, 2016.

Glassman, Steve. *It Happened on the Santa Fe Trail*. Twodot, 2008.

Hearst Castle, California State Parks

The Historic Rios-Caledonia Adobe, Rios-Caledonia Adobe

La Purisima Mission State Historic Park Self-Guided Tour, California State Parks

La Purisima Mission State Historic Park, California State Parks

Map and Guide to Mission San Juan Capistrano, Mission San Juan Capistrano

Marcy, Randolph, *The Prairie Traveler, 1859*.

Margolin, Malcolm. *Life In A California Mission*. Heyday Books, 1989.

Maritime Museum of San Diego, Maritime Museum of San Diego

Mayo, Matthew P. *Haunted Old West: Phantom Cowboys, Spirit-Filled Saloons, Mystical Mine Camps, and Spectral Indians*. Globe Pequot Press, 2012.

McLaughlin, David *Soldiers, Scoundrels, Poets & Priests*, Pentacle Press, 2018.

Mission Basilica San Buenaventura, Mission Basilica San Buenaventura

Mission Basilica San Diego De Alcala, Mission Basilica San Diego De Alcala

Mission San Antonio De Padua Visitors Map and Historical Chronicle, Mission San Antonio De Padua

Mission San Gabriel Archangel, San Gabriel Mission, 2015.

Mission San Luis Obispo de Tolosa, Mission San Luis Obispo de Tolosa

Mission San Luis Rey, Mission San Luis Rey

Old Mission San Miguel Archangel, Mission San Miguel Arcangel, 2006.

Rios-Caledonia Adobe, Rios-Caledonia Adobe

Rutter, Michael. *Bedside Book of Bad Girls: Outlaw Women of the American West*. Farcountry Press, 2008.

Scott, Robert. *Plain Enemies: Best True Stories of the Frontier West*. Caxton Printers, 1995.

Senate, Richard. *Ghosts of the California Missions*. Shoreline Press, 2011.

Wagner, Tricia Martineau. *It Happened on the Oregon Trail: Remarkable Events That Shaped History*. GPP, 2014.

Welcome to El Presidio De Santa Barbara State Historic Park, Santa Barbara Trust for Historic Preservation.

Welcome to San Miguel Chapel, San Miguel Chapel

Welcome to the Living Old Mission Santa Barbara, Mission Santa Barbara

The World Famous Whaley House, Whaley House

Index

Referenced by Sections

Hunter-Leggett Military Complex-see Mission San Antonio de Padua

Huntington Library-see Pasadena

I

Inca-see San Diego

Island of the Blue Dolphins-see Santa Barbara Mission

J

James, Frank and Jesse-see Mission San Miguel Archangel

Jamestown-see San Diego

Jayme, Father Luis-see Mission San Diego de Alcala

Joke glass-see Los Angeles

Juana Maria-see Santa Barbara Mission

K

King Louis IX of France-see Mission San Luis Rey de Francia

King of Missions-see Mission San Luis Rey de Francia

L

La Brea Tar Pits-see Los Angeles

Lasuen, Father Fermin-see Mission San Luis Rey de Francia

Life Magazine-see San Diego

About the Author

Julie Bettendorf is a world traveler with a degree in archaeology and a background in history. She has traveled extensively throughout Egypt, Central America, South America, Europe, and the United Kingdom, visiting archaeological and historical sites all along the way.

Currently, Julie is traveling around the US visiting ghost towns, ancient rock art sites, and archaeological wonders as part of research for her ongoing historical travel series entitled ***Wandering Woman***. Wandering Woman is a set of state-by-state guides, full of photographs, historical anecdotes, and unique tips to help other women travel and explore solo across the US by car. Julie enjoys writing freelance blogs, traveling frequently with her two adult children, and hiking outdoors with her faithful dog companion Rosie.

Also by Julie Bettendorf

Wandering Woman: Southern California is the eleventh book in the ***Wandering Woman Travel Series***. The first ten books of ***Wandering Woman: Montana***, ***Utah, Colorado, Oregon, Washington, Idaho, Wyoming, Arizona, New Mexico, and Nevada*** are available in ebook and paperback.

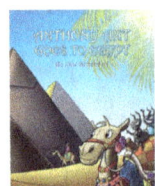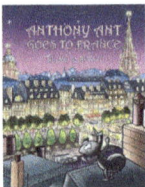

Julie has published two children's books in an ongoing, beautifully illustrated travel series entitled ***Anthony Ant Goes to France*** and ***Anthony Ant Goes to Egypt***.

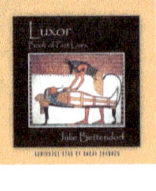

She has also published a work of historical fiction entitled ***Luxor: Book of Past Lives*** which has recently been released as an audiobook, read by renowned narrator Barry Shannon.